Murder Hornets Invade Honeybee Colonies

By Susan H. Gray

21st Century
Junior Library

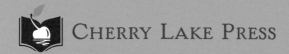

CHERRY LAKE PRESS

Published in the United States of America by Cherry Lake Publishing Group
Ann Arbor, Michigan
www.cherrylakepublishing.com

Reading Adviser: Beth Walker Gambro, MS, Ed., Reading Consultant, Yorkville, IL
Book Designer: Melinda Millward

Photo Credits: © KEA1977/Shutterstock.com, cover; © /Shutterstock.com, 4; © Washington State
Department of Agriculture, 6, 8, 12, 14, 16, 18, 20; © Daniel Prudek/Shutterstock.com, 10

Cherry Lake Press is an imprint of Cherry Lake Publishing Group.

Library of Congress Cataloging-in-Publication Data

Names: Gray, Susan Heinrichs, author.
Title: Murder hornets invade honeybee colonies / by Susan H. Gray.
Description: Ann Arbor, Michigan : Cherry Lake Publishing, 2021. | Series: Invasive species science :
    tracking and controlling | Includes index. | Audience: Grades 2-3
Identifiers: LCCN 2021004865 (print) | LCCN 2021004866 (ebook) | ISBN 9781534187009
    (hardcover) | ISBN 9781534188402 (paperback) | ISBN 9781534189805 (pdf) |
    ISBN 9781534191204 (ebook)
Subjects: LCSH: Hornets—Control—Juvenile literature. | Introduced insects—Juvenile literature. |
    Invasive species—Control—Islands of the Pacific—Juvenile literature.
Classification: LCC QL568.V5 G73 2021 (print) | LCC QL568.V5 (ebook) | DDC 595.79/8—dc23
LC record available at https://lccn.loc.gov/2021004865
LC ebook record available at https://lccn.loc.gov/2021004866

Cherry Lake Publishing Group would like to acknowledge the work of the Partnership for 21st
Century Learning, a Network of Battelle for Kids. Please visit http://www.battelleforkids.org/
networks/p21 for more information.

Printed in the United States of America
Corporate Graphics

CONTENTS

At 2 inches (5 centimeters) in length, it is the world's largest hornet.

Mysterious Visitors

It's a perfect October morning. The forest air is clean and crisp. Orange and yellow leaves flutter to the ground. Inside one tree is a nest of Asian giant **hornets**, also called "murder hornets." Some are spitting up food they swallowed hours ago. Others are feeding on it. Still others are just resting. Outside, though, a mysterious scene is unfolding.

Regular beekeeping suits aren't strong enough
to withstand murder hornet stings.

People in big rubbery suits surround the tree. They use foam to seal up any nest openings they find. They wrap the tree in **cellophane** and then leave.

A few days pass, and the people return with a chainsaw. The tree ends up in a large, very cold room. People count, measure, and take pictures. What is going on?

Make a Guess!

Cold weather makes some animals move slowly. Why would people store the hornet tree in a cold room?

Inside the nest, murder hornet **larvae** cocoon themselves.

An Alarming Discovery

It's October 2020. The people are scientists in the state of Washington. They are the first ones to find an Asian giant hornet nest in the United States.

Look!

Find pictures online of **cicada** killers. How are they different from murder hornets?

About one-third of your food comes from crops pollinated by honeybees.

Murder hornets are an **invasive species**. They destroy honeybees. They move into beehives and kill the adults. Hornets then chew young, developing bees into mush. When they return to their nest, the mush becomes food for other hornets.

The death of honeybees is tragic. Bees make honey and wax, which have many uses. But their most important job is **pollination**. As honeybees visit flowers, they transfer **pollen** from one flower to the next. If pollen sticks to the right flower part, a seed forms. Gardeners and farmers count on honeybees.

In order to catch a murder hornet, scientists set up traps with juice.

Hornets Get Technical

In 2019, the hornets were discovered in Canada, very close to Washington. Scientists in Washington soon heard about it. They knew the hornets might show up in their area. Soon, a Washington **resident** reported an unusual hornet on his land. Experts compared it to **native** hornets. Their worst fear had come true. Asian giant hornets had arrived in the United States.

Trackers allow researchers to follow animals' movements.
They can even lead scientists to animals' nests.

The scientists asked everyone to be on the lookout for the invaders. They talked to news reporters. They posted pictures of the hornet online. They set up a hotline for people to call with hornet sightings.

They also contacted **engineers** at the University of Washington. Some of those engineers were developing tiny radio trackers for small animals to wear.

Think!

Scientists wanted people to be aware of the hornets. But they did not want anyone to worry needlessly. So they put photos online of murder hornets next to native hornets. Why would they do this?

Scientists first attempted to glue the tracker directly onto the hornet.

One engineering student was building such devices. But could he make one to fit a hornet? The device must have a computer chip, an antenna, and a battery. How much weight could a hornet carry? How do you stick a tracker on an **insect**? How many hours of battery power does it need? Where does the antenna go so it's not in the hornet's way?

Ask Questions!

A tracker cannot be placed just anywhere on an animal. It must not **interfere** with the animal's life. Where would you put a tracker on a turtle? An eagle? Or on a grasshopper?

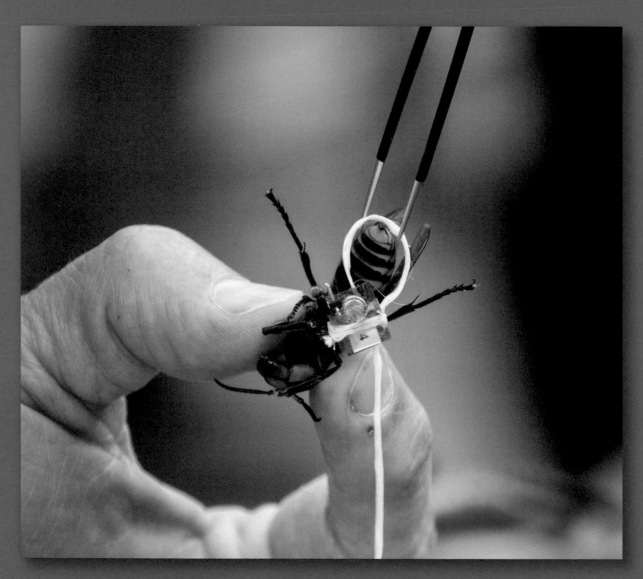

Dental floss is light and won't slip.

A Great Solution

The student could not mount the device on the hornet's back. The insect would be top-heavy and roll over in flight. So he decided to hang it from the hornet's waist. The antenna would trail out behind as the hornet flew. A small, light battery could last 12 hours. A hornet would probably lead scientists to its nest within that time. The whole thing would be tied on with dental floss.

The Washington State Department of Agriculture team smiles after the first successful extraction of hornets.

The device worked perfectly! The hornet led scientists right to its home. Within days, the nest was down. Scientists opened up the tree. They were counting hornets and studying the nest.

The scientists' work is not done. They are still talking to reporters. People are still answering the hotline. And engineers are still working on better ways to chase these new invaders.

GLOSSARY

cellophane (SELL-uh-fayn) a clear, waterproof material used to wrap food or other objects

cicada (suh-KAY-duh) a large, noisy flying insect

engineers (en-juh-NEERZ) people who design and build machines, bridges, computers, and other structures and devices

hornets (HOR-nits) large, stinging members of the wasp group of insects

insect (IN-sekt) an animal with six legs, no backbone, and three main body parts

interfere (in-tur-FEER) to slow down or get in the way of something

invasive (in-VAY-sihv) not native, but entering by force or by accident and spreading quickly

larvae (lahr-vee) young insect hatchlings

native (NAY-tihv) occurring naturally in a particular place

pollen (PAHL-uhn) a powdery material in the flowers of many plants

pollination (PAHL-uh-NAY-shun) the transfer of pollen from one flower part to another

resident (REZ-uh-duhnt) a person who lives in a certain place

species (SPEE-sheez) a particular kind of plant or animal